Will Rogers

Terry Barber

FIRST
NATIONS
SERIES

Will Rogers is published by
Grass Roots Press, a division of Literacy Services of Canada Ltd.

www.grassrootsbooks.net

ACKNOWLEDGEMENTS

We acknowledge the financial support of the Government of Canada through the Canada Book Fund (CBF) for our publishing activities.

Produced with the assistance of
the Government of Alberta, Alberta
Multimedia Development Fund.

Alberta
Government

Editor: Dr. Pat Campbell
Image research: Dr. Pat Campbell
Book design: Lara Minja, Lime Design Inc.

Library and Archives Canada Cataloguing in Publication

Barber, Terry, date, author
        Will Rogers / Terry Barber.

ISBN 978–1–77153–044–6 (bound)

        1. Rogers, Will, 1879–1935. 2. Entertainers—United States—
Biography. 3. Humorists, American—Biography. 4. Readers for
new literates. I. Title.

PE1126.N43B36792 2015   428.6'2   C2015–902588–5

Printed in Canada.

Contents

Will says goodbye to his wife Betty.

Will's Last Smile

The year is 1935. Betty stands in the field. Betty watches the airplane. The airplane climbs into the sky. Betty's husband, Will, sits in the plane. Will smiles. Betty sees his smile. Betty never sees Will smile again.

A young Will (left) and a friend.

Early Years

Will Rogers is born in 1879. Will's parents are part Cherokee. Will's family lives in Indian Territory. Will has seven older brothers and sisters. He likes everybody. The only thing Will dislikes is school. Will and school never get along.

Today, the Indian Territory is part of Oklahoma.

Will is born in this house.

Early Years

Will's family live on a large ranch.
Their home is large. Will's world is not
like today's world. Cattle **roam** freely.
Will rides his horses freely. He has
many horses and loves them all.
Will's childhood is carefree.

Will's parents own 20,000 acres of land.

Will practises his roping.

Early Years

To Will, riding a horse is as easy
as walking. Will always rides with
a lasso. From his horse, Will ropes
cattle. In fact, Will ropes anything that
moves. Off his horse, Will does rope
tricks with his lasso.

Will
calls himself
an Indian
cowboy.

Will wears his "Cherokee Kid" outfit.
1903.

Will Sees the World

Will drops out of school in 1898. He is 18 years old. Free at last, Will travels the world. He works as a cowboy in Texas and South America. He works as a trick roper in Australia. Will works for a circus in South Africa.

Will is named the "Cherokee Kid" in the circus.

Will throws ropes on a vaudeville stage.

Will Sees the World

Will returns to the United States in 1904. Will is broke and needs to find work. He finds work on a **vaudeville** stage.

Vaudeville has all sorts of acts from singers to dancers. Will's roping act is unlike any other act.

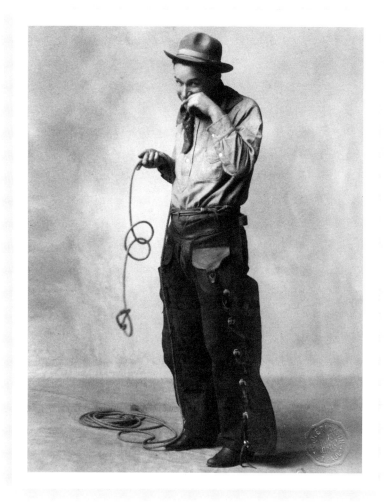

Will in a funny **pose.**

Will Sees the World

In 1906, Will takes his vaudeville act
to Europe. People love to watch Will
and his horse. They love Will's charm
and sense of fun. Will's life is exciting,
but he is lonely. He feels homesick.
Will asks Betty to marry him.

Will meets
Betty Blake
in 1900.

Betty and Will with their children.

Will's Family

In 1908, Will marries Betty. By 1915, Betty and Will have three children. Bill is the oldest. Next comes Mary. Jimmy is the youngest. Will loves his children. Will is a fine father. Betty is a great mother. Their family life is strong.

A lily rests on a gravestone.

Will's Family

A fourth child, Freddy, is born to
Betty and Will in 1918. Freddy dies
when he is 23 months old. Will and
Betty are so sad over their son's death.
Will finds comfort in his work.

Freddy
dies from
diphtheria.

Will writes and ropes at the same time.

Will's Family

Will is one of those people who must move. Will can't even sit still between the main course and dessert. Will often practises roping tricks between courses. Betty doesn't mind because Will is just being Will.

Will spends lots of time with his children.
Left to right: Will, Bill, Mary, and Jim.

Will's Family

Will says he will never grow up. Will says that Betty is raising four children. Three are by birth and one is by marriage. Will travels a lot because of his work. Will's children miss their father. Betty misses him too.

Will throws a rope around his cast.

Will's Jokes

Will's vaudeville act becomes famous in the United States. People love Will's roping tricks. Then, one day, Will talks during his act. Soon, Will does more talking than roping. Will tells stories. Will makes jokes. Will makes jokes mostly about politics.

Will and the President's wife, Eleanor Roosevelt.

Will's Jokes

Will even jokes about presidents.
Will's jokes aren't mean. Will is friends
with many of the people he jokes
about.

Will jokes about himself. Will says he
talks too much. Will says he talks so
much he could be a politician.

Will usually has a smile on his face.

Will's Jokes

Will also jokes about the way he looks. Will says that some people want to improve their looks. Not Will. "I want people to know why I look this way. I've travelled a long way. And some of the roads weren't paved."

Will and "Dizzy" Dean at the World Series.
1934.

Will's Fame

America falls in love with Will Rogers. Will tells the truth in a fun way. He also has common sense. "Don't let yesterday use up too much of today," Will says. People see themselves and the world through Will.

Will delivers his radio program.

Will's Fame

By the early 1920s, Will is as famous
as anyone in America. Will has many
talents. Will is a movie actor. Will
writes for newspapers. Will has a
radio program. Will is America's
best-loved son. None of this fame
changes Will.

Will writes a newspaper story in his car.

Will's Fame

Will's fame helps people through the **Great Depression**. Through Will, people escape. People watch his movies and have a laugh. Will's newspaper words cause people to think. Will is the most popular newspaper writer in America.

Will stars in 47 silent movies and 21 sound movies.

Will helps the **Red Cross** in Arkansas.
1931.

Will's Fame

Will loves people. Will treats all people with respect. Will wants all people to have good lives. When bad things happen, Will wants to help. People come to hear Will speak. Will gives the money from some of his talks to people in need.

Will plays "shake a paw" with a dog.

Will's Fame

Will says: "I never met a man I didn't like." Will loves animals as much as he loves people. Will treats humans and animals the same, with kindness. Will believes a dog is a friend for life.

Will stands in front of an airplane.

Will's Fame

Will changes with the times. By the early 1930s, much of his travel is by airplane. Will can now travel to far-off places quickly. Will sees much of the world by airplane. Will wants to see Alaska by airplane.

The Indian cowboy lives on.

Will's Words
Live On

Will's smile is lost to the world on August 15, 1935. The plane he is on crashes in Alaska. Both Will and the pilot die.

Today, streets are named after Will. People visit statues of Will. To this day, people still quote Will. The Indian cowboy lives on.

Glossary

diphtheria: a disease that can cause death.

Great Depression: a time of high unemployment, falling stock prices, and low wages.

pose: the way one stands or sits before someone takes their photo.

Red Cross: a group that helps people in need.

roam: to move about over a large area.

vaudeville: a number of stage acts that includes comedians, singers, dancers, musicians, animals, etc.

Talking About the Book

What did you learn about Will Rogers?

"Don't let yesterday use up too much of today."
What does this quote mean?

Why did America fall in love with Will Rogers?

How did Will respond to fame?

Do you think you would respond to fame
in the same way?

Picture Credits

Photographs courtesy of Will Rogers Memorial Museum.